GW01237590

MASTERING CORE M

OCR SYLLABUS

YOUR FAST TRACK

TO A-LEVEL SUCCESS

THE MATHS CLINIC

Copyright © 2016 The Maths Clinic

ISBN-10:1517037115
ISBN-13:978-1517037116

DEDICATED TO THE SERIOUS STUDENT

"It takes a lot of hard work to make something simple"

-Steve Jobs-

CONTENTS

THE M.T.V. METHOD
Memorise . Test . Validate

Drawing from years of teaching Mathematics, The Maths Clinic has devised a foolproof method to master mathematical concepts for success in exams.

Armed with pen and notepad, follow this three-step M.T.V. method for each chapter:

A set of key points encapsulates each mathematical topic. Take time to commit this key list to memory. The success of your exam preparation depends on this step. Master the basics and you will master Mathematics.

MEMORISE

The test page checks your assimilation of the key points for the chapter. Associated with each key point is a key question. Work through the test questions diligently.

TEST

Check the answers to all the key questions here. The answer page includes step by step working of each question.

VALIDATE

We recommend a thorough exam preparation to include the following:
Step 1: Master the key points using the M.T.V. Method.
Step 2: Answer at least five past exam question papers completely and within the prescribed time

1. INDICES

1.1 KEY POINTS

1. $a^m \times a^n = a^{m+n}$

2. $\dfrac{a^m}{a^n} = a^{m-n}$

3. $(a^m)^n = a^{mn}$

4. $a^{-n} = \dfrac{1}{a^n}$

5. $a^{\frac{1}{n}} = \sqrt[n]{a}$

6. $a^{\frac{m}{n}} = \sqrt[n]{a^m}$

7. $a^0 = 1$

8. Memorise the squares of all numbers from 1 to 15.

9. Memorise the cubes of all numbers from 1 to 10.

1.2 TEST YOURSELF

1. $a^m \times a^n =$ $2^5 \times 2^3 =$

2. $\dfrac{a^m}{a^n} =$ $\dfrac{3^7}{3^4} =$

3. $(a^m)^n$ $(5^2)^2 =$

4. $a^{-n} =$ $2^{-3} =$

5. $a^{\frac{1}{n}} =$ $9^{\frac{1}{2}} =$

6. $a^{\frac{m}{n}} =$ $27^{\frac{2}{3}} =$

7. $a^0 =$ $15^0 =$

8. List the squares of all numbers from 1 to 15.

9. List the cubes of all numbers from 1 to 10.

1.3 ANSWERS

1. $2^5 \times 2^3 = 2^8 = 256$

2. $\frac{3^7}{3^4} = 3^3 = 27$

3. $(5^2)^2 = 5^4 = 625$

4. $2^{-3} = \frac{1}{2^3} = \frac{1}{8}$

5. $9^{\frac{1}{2}} = \sqrt{9} = 3$

6. $27^{\frac{2}{3}} = (\sqrt[3]{27})^2 = 3^2 = 9$

7. $15^0 = 1$

8.

$1^2 = 1$	$6^2 = 36$	$11^2 = 121$
$2^2 = 4$	$7^2 = 49$	$12^2 = 144$
$3^2 = 9$	$8^2 = 64$	$13^2 = 169$
$4^2 = 16$	$9^2 = 81$	$14^2 = 196$
$5^2 = 25$	$10^2 = 100$	$15^2 = 225$

9.

$1^3 = 1$	$4^3 = 64$	$6^3 = 216$	$9^3 = 729$
$2^3 = 8$	$5^3 = 125$	$7^3 = 343$	$10^3 = 1000$
$3^3 = 27$	$6^3 = 216$	$8^3 = 512$	

2. SURDS

2.1 KEY POINTS

1. A surd is a square root of a prime number.

2. $\sqrt{ab} = \sqrt{a} \times \sqrt{b}$

3. $\sqrt{a} \times \sqrt{a} = \sqrt{a \times a} = a$

4. $\sqrt{\dfrac{a}{b}} = \dfrac{\sqrt{a}}{\sqrt{b}}$

5. To rationalise fractions in the form $\dfrac{1}{\sqrt{a}}$, multiply numerator and denominator by $\sqrt{a}$

6. To rationalise fractions in the form $\dfrac{1}{a+\sqrt{b}}$, multiply numerator and denominator by $a - \sqrt{b}$

7. To rationalise fractions in the form $\dfrac{1}{a-\sqrt{b}}$, multiply numerator and denominator by $a + \sqrt{b}$

8. Difference of two squares:
    $(a + b)(a - b) = a^2 - b^2$

9. Expansion using FOIL:

    Multiply in **FOIL** order

    > **F**irst terms

    > **O**uter terms

    > **I**nner terms

    > **L**ast terms

    $\left(5 + \sqrt{3}\right)\left(2 + \sqrt{3}\right)$

    $= 10 + 5\sqrt{3} + 2\sqrt{3} + 3$

    $= 13 + 7\sqrt{3}$

2.2 TEST YOURSELF

1.   List all the prime numbers between 1 and 10.

2.   Define a surd.

      Give 5 examples.

3. $\sqrt{ab} =$ $\sqrt{15} =$

      $\sqrt{a} \times \sqrt{a} =$ $\sqrt{11} \times \sqrt{11} =$

4. $\sqrt{\dfrac{a}{b}} =$ $\sqrt{\dfrac{5}{7}} =$

5.   Difference of two squares:

      $(a + b)(a - b) =$

      Evaluate:

      $\left(5 + \sqrt{19}\right)\left(5 - \sqrt{19}\right) =$

6.   Define FOIL expansion.

      Expand and simplify using FOIL:

      $\left(2 + \sqrt{5}\right)\left(1 + 2\sqrt{5}\right) =$

7.   To rationalise fractions in the form $\dfrac{1}{\sqrt{a}}$, multiply

      numerator and denominator by _____.

      Rationalise:

      $\dfrac{25}{\sqrt{5}} =$

8. To rationalise fractions in the form $\frac{1}{a+\sqrt{b}}$, multiply

    numerator and denominator by _____.

    Rationalise:

    $$\frac{1}{3+\sqrt{7}} =$$

9. To rationalise fractions in the form $\frac{1}{a-\sqrt{b}}$, multiply

    numerator and denominator by _____.

    Rationalise:

    $$\frac{4}{3-\sqrt{5}} =$$

10. Express the following in surd form $a\sqrt{b}$

    $\sqrt{32} =$

    $\sqrt{45} =$

    $\sqrt{72} =$

    $\sqrt{12} + \sqrt{75} =$

11. Rationalise and simplify

    $$\frac{\sqrt{7} - \sqrt{2}}{\sqrt{7} + \sqrt{2}} =$$

12. Rationalise and simplify

    $$\frac{5\sqrt{2}}{3+\sqrt{2}} =$$

2.3 ANSWERS

1.   Primes between 1 and 10 are 2, 3, 5 and 7.

2.   Examples of surds: $\sqrt{2}, \sqrt{3}, \sqrt{5}, \sqrt{7}, \sqrt{11}$

3. $\sqrt{15} = \sqrt{3} \times \sqrt{5}$

$$\sqrt{11} \times \sqrt{11} = \sqrt{11 \times 11} = \sqrt{11}^2 = 11$$

4. $\sqrt{\dfrac{5}{7}} = \dfrac{\sqrt{5}}{\sqrt{7}}$

5. $\left(5 + \sqrt{19}\right)\left(5 - \sqrt{19}\right)$

$$= \left(5^2 - \sqrt{19}^2\right)$$

$$= 25 - 19$$

$$= 6$$

6. $\left(2 + \sqrt{5}\right)\left(1 + 2\sqrt{5}\right)$

$$= \left(2.1 + 2.2\sqrt{5} + \sqrt{5}.1 + \sqrt{5}.2\sqrt{5}\right)$$

$$= \left(2 + 4\sqrt{5} + \sqrt{5} + 10\right)$$

$$= \left(12 + 5\sqrt{5}\right)$$

7. $\dfrac{25}{\sqrt{5}}$

$$= \frac{25 \times \sqrt{5}}{\sqrt{5} \times \sqrt{5}}$$

$$= \frac{25 \times \sqrt{5}}{5}$$

$$= 5\sqrt{5}$$

8. $\dfrac{1}{3+\sqrt{7}}$

$$= \frac{1}{3+\sqrt{7}} \times \frac{(3-\sqrt{7})}{(3-\sqrt{7})}$$

$$= \frac{1.(3-\sqrt{7})}{(3+\sqrt{7})(3-\sqrt{7})}$$

$$= \frac{(3-\sqrt{7})}{(9-7)}$$

$$= \frac{(3-\sqrt{7})}{2}$$

9. $\dfrac{4}{3-\sqrt{5}}$

$$= \frac{4}{(3-\sqrt{5})} \times \frac{(3+\sqrt{5})}{(3+\sqrt{5})}$$

$$= \frac{4.(3+\sqrt{5})}{(3-\sqrt{5}))(3+\sqrt{5})}$$

$$= \frac{12+4\sqrt{5}}{(9-5)}$$

$$= \frac{12+4\sqrt{5}}{4}$$

$$= 3+\sqrt{5}$$

10. $\sqrt{32} = \sqrt{2\times2\times2\times2\times2} = 4\sqrt{2}$

$\sqrt{45} = \sqrt{3\times3\times5} = 3\sqrt{5}$

$\sqrt{72} = \sqrt{2\times2\times2\times3\times3} = 6\sqrt{2}$

$\sqrt{12} + \sqrt{75}$

$$= \sqrt{2 \times 2 \times 3} + \sqrt{3 \times 5 \times 5}$$

$$= 2\sqrt{3} + 5\sqrt{3}$$

$$= 7\sqrt{3}$$

11. $\dfrac{\sqrt{7} - \sqrt{2}}{\sqrt{7} + \sqrt{2}}$

$$= \frac{\sqrt{7} - \sqrt{2}}{\sqrt{7} + \sqrt{2}} \times \frac{\sqrt{7} - \sqrt{2}}{\sqrt{7} - \sqrt{2}}$$

$$= \frac{(\sqrt{7} - \sqrt{2})(\sqrt{7} - \sqrt{2})}{(\sqrt{7} + \sqrt{2})(\sqrt{7} - \sqrt{2})}$$

$$= \frac{\left(7 - 2\sqrt{14} + 2\right)}{7 - 2}$$

$$= \frac{9 - 2\sqrt{14}}{5}$$

12. $\dfrac{5\sqrt{2}}{3 + \sqrt{2}}$

$$= \frac{5\sqrt{2}}{3 + \sqrt{2}} \times \frac{3 - \sqrt{2}}{3 - \sqrt{2}}$$

$$= \frac{5\sqrt{2}\left(3 - \sqrt{2}\right)}{(3 + \sqrt{2})(3 - \sqrt{2})}$$

$$= \frac{15\sqrt{2} - 10}{(9 - 2)} = \frac{15\sqrt{2} - 10}{7}$$

3. FACTORISATION

3.1 KEY POINTS

Factorisation is the decomposition of an algebraic expression into factors which when multiplied together return the original expression.

Case 1:

Factorise by taking out the common factors in an expression.

     a. $6x + 18 = 3(2x + 6)$
     b. $15x - 20 = 5(3x - 4)$
     c. $5x^2 - 10x = 5x(x - 2)$

Case 2:

Factorise a two-term expression with a difference of 2 squares using the following:

$$a^2 - b^2 = (a + b)(a - b)$$

     a. $x^2 - 64 = (x + 8)(x - 8)$
     b. $25x^2 - 4y^2$
     $= (5x + 2y)(5x - 2y)$
     c. $4y^2 - 1 = (2y + 1)(2y - 1)$

Case 3:

Factorise a quadratic function of the form

$ax^2 + bx + c$ where a, b and c are constants and $a \neq 0$ using the **Cross Method**.

$$x^2 - 2x - 15$$
$$= (x + 3)(x - 5)$$

Steps for Factorising: $x^2 - 2x - 15$

i)   Factorise the first term x^2 and place factors at the top left and bottom left arms of the cross.
      $$x^2 = (x) \times (x)$$

ii)   Factorise the third term -15 and place factors at the top right and bottom right arms of the cross.
      $$-15 = (+3) \times (-5)$$

iii) Cross multiply terms along arms and add the results to get the middle term.
      $$(+3)(x) + (-5)(x) = -2x$$

      If the middle term is not obtained, try other factors.

      By reading across, we get the solution.

      $$x^2 - 2x - 15 = (x + 3)(x - 5)$$

Factorise $3x^2 + 5x - 2$ using the Cross Method

$$= (3x - 1)(x + 2)$$

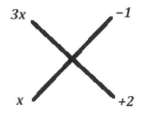

3.2 TEST YOURSELF

1. Define Factorisation.
2. Name the 3 methods used.
3. $a^2 - b^2 =$
4. Case 1 Factorisation

   (Extract common factors)

   i) $2x^2 - 4x =$
   ii) $7x - 21x^2 =$

5. Case 2 Factorisation

   (Difference of two squares)

   i) $1 - 49x^2 =$
   ii) $16x^2 - 25 =$

6. Case 1 & Case 2 Combination:

   i) $x^3 - 36x =$
   ii) $3x^2 - 12 =$

7. Case 3 Factorisation

   (Cross Method)

   i) $x^2 + 5x + 6 =$
   ii) $2x^2 + 3x + 1 =$

8. Case 1 & Case 3 Combination:

   i) $x^3 + 4x^2 - 21x =$
   ii) $2x^3 + 4x^2 - 16x =$

3.3 ANSWERS

1.   Check Key Points for answer.
2.   Check Key Points for answer.
3.   Check Key Points for answer.

4.   Case 1 Factorisation

   (Extract common factors)

   i) $2x^2 - 4x = 2x(x - 2)$
   ii) $7x - 21x^2 = 7x(1 - 3x)$

5.   Case 2 Factorisation

   (Difference of two squares)

   i) $1 - 49x^2$
        $= (1 + 7x)(1 - 7x)$
   ii) $16x^2 - 25$
        $= (4x + 5)(4x - 5)$

6.   Case 1 & Case 2 Combination:
   i) $x^3 - 36x$

        $= x(x^2 - 36)$

        $= x(x + 6)(x - 6)$

   ii) $3x^2 - 12$

        $= 3(x^2 - 4)$

        $= 3(x + 2)(x - 2)$

7.   Case 3 Factorisation

   (Cross Method)

   i) $x^2 + 5x + 6$
        $= (x + 3)(x + 2)$

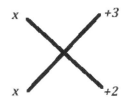

ii) $2x^2 + 3x + 1$
     $= (2x + 1)(x + 1)$

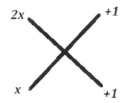

8.   Case 1 & Case 3 Combination:

   i) $x^3 + 4x^2 - 21x$
   $= x(x^2 + 4x - 21)$
   $= x(x + 7)(x - 3)$

ii) $2x^3 + 4x^2 - 16x$
   $= 2x(x^2 + 2x - 8)$
   $= 2x(x + 4)(x - 2)$

4. ALGEBRA

4.1 KEY POINTS

1. **Expansion facts:**
   i) $(x + y)^2$
   $= x^2 + 2xy + y^2$
   $(5x + 4)^2$
   $= 25x^2 + 40x + 16$
   ii) $(x - y)^2$
   $= x^2 - 2xy + y^2$
   $(x - 2)^2$
   $= x^2 - 4x + 4$

2. **Change the Subject of the Formula:**

   <u>Rules:</u>

   a)   Swap sides to get the required subject on the left hand side (LHS) of the equals sign.

   b)   Start moving non-subject variables from the LHS of the equals sign to the right hand side (RHS) by reversing each operation.

   Addition⟺Subtraction

   Multiplication⟺Division

   Square⟺Square root

   Cube⟺Cube root

   Given that

   $V = \pi r^2 h$, make r the subject of the formula.

   $\pi r^2 h = V$ (Swap sides)

   $r^2 = \dfrac{V}{\pi h}$ (Cross divide by πh)

   $r = \sqrt{\dfrac{V}{\pi h}}$ (Find square root)

4.2 TEST YOURSELF

1. Expand:
   - i) $(x + y)^2 =$
   - ii) $(x - y)^2 =$

2. Expand:
   - i) $(9x + 1)^2 =$
   - ii) $(4 - 7x)^2 =$

3. Given that $y = mx + c$, make x the subject of the formula.

4. Given that $s = ut + \frac{1}{2}at^2$, make a the subject of the formula.

5. Given that $y + 3xy = 2 - xy$, make x the subject of the formula.

6. Given that $y = \sqrt{x - 5}$, make x the subject of the formula.

4.3 ANSWERS

1.
   i) Check Key Points for answer.

   ii) Check Key Points for answer.

2.   Expand:
   i) $(9x + 1)^2$

   $= (9x)^2 + 2.9x.1 + 1^2$

   $= 81x^2 + 18x + 1$

   ii) $(4 - 7x)^2$

   $= 4^2 - 2.4.7x + (7x)^2$

   $= 16 - 56x + 49x^2$

3. $y = mx + c$ (x)

   $\therefore mx + c = y$

   $mx = y - c$

   $x = \dfrac{y - c}{m}$

4. $s = ut + \frac{1}{2}at^2$ (a)

   $ut + \dfrac{1}{2}at^2 = s$

   $\dfrac{1}{2}at^2 = s - ut$

   $at^2 = 2(s - ut)$

   $a = \dfrac{2(s - ut)}{t^2}$

5. $y + 3xy = 2 - xy \quad (x)$

$3xy + xy = 2 - y$

$4xy = 2 - y$

$x = \dfrac{2 - y}{4y}$

6. $y = \sqrt{x - 5} \quad (x)$

$\sqrt{x - 5} = y$

$\left(\sqrt{x - 5}\right)^2 = y^2$

$x - 5 = y^2$

$x = y^2 + 5$

5. QUADRATIC EQUATIONS

5.1 KEY POINTS

The general form of a quadratic equation is:

$f(x) = ax^2 + bx + c = 0$ where a, b and c are constants and $a \neq 0$. We solve a quadratic equation by finding the roots or solutions for x.

1.   Solving a quadratic equation

Method 1 by Factorisation.

Factorise the quadratic and equate each factor to 0.

Case 1 (Extract common factors)

$x^2 - 3x = 0$

$x(x - 3) = 0$

$\therefore x = 0 \; and \; (x - 3) = 0$

$Solutions: x = 0, x = 3$

Case 2 (Difference of two squares)

$x^2 - 4 = 0$

$(x + 2)(x - 2) = 0$

$\therefore (x + 2) = 0 \text{ and } (x - 2) = 0$

$Solutions: x = \pm 2$

Case 3 (Cross Method)

$x^2 + 3x + 2 = 0$

$(x + 2)(x + 1) = 0$

$\therefore (x + 2) = 0 \; and \; (x + 1) = 0$

$Solutions: x = -1, x = -2$

2. Solving a quadratic equation

Method 2 by completing the square

$$x^2 + bx = (x + \frac{b}{2})^2 - (\frac{b}{2})^2$$

$$\therefore x^2 + 8x$$

$$= (x + 4)^2 - (4)^2$$

$$= (x + 4)^2 - 16$$

This method is used to solve the quadratic equation

$$x^2 + 8x + 12 = 0$$

$$x^2 + 8x = -12$$

$$(x + 4)^2 - 16 = -12 \text{ (By completing the square)}$$

$$(x + 4)^2 = -12 + 16$$

$$(x + 4)^2 = 4$$

$$(x + 4) = \pm2$$

$$x_1 = 2 - 4 = -2$$

$$x_2 = -2 - 4 = -6$$

3. Solving a quadratic equation

Method 3 by Using the Formula

For $ax^2 + bx + c = 0$

$$x = \frac{-b \pm \sqrt{b^2 - 4ac}}{2a}$$

This method gives x in surd form.

$x^2 + 3x + 2 = 0$

$a = 1, b = 3, c = 2$

$$x = \frac{-3 \pm \sqrt{9-8}}{2}$$

$$= \frac{-3 \pm 1}{2} = -1, -2$$

5.2 TEST YOURSELF

1. What are the 3 methods of solving a quadratic equation?
2. Complete the square:

$$x^2 + bx =$$

3. For $ax^2 + bx + c = 0$ give the formula for the 2 solutions of x (usually in surd form)

$$x =$$

4. Using Method 1, solve the quadratic equations:

   a) $x^3 - 9x = 0$

   b) $x^3 - 7x^2 + 10x = 0$

5. Complete the square for the following:
   a) $x^2 - 8x =$
   b) $2x^2 - 20x =$

6. Using Method 2, solve the quadratic equations:
   a) $x^2 + 2x - 8 = 0$
   b) $x^2 + 12x + 27 = 0$

7. Using Method 3, solve the quadratic equations and give the solutions in surd form:
   a) $2x^2 - 4x - 3 = 0$
   b) $x^2 - 2x - 4 = 0$

5.3   ANSWERS

1. Check Key Points for answer.
2. Check Key Points for answer.
3. Check Key Points for answer.

4.

a) $x^3 - 9x = 0$

$x(x^2 - 9) = 0$

$x(x + 3)(x - 3) = 0$

$\therefore x = 0, x = 3, x = -3$

b) $x^3 - 7x^2 + 10x = 0$

$x(x^2 - 7x + 10) = 0$

$x(x - 5)(x - 2) = 0$

$x = 0, x = 5, x = 2$

5.

a) $x^2 - 8x$

$= (x - 4)^2 - (-4)^2$

$= (x - 4)^2 - 16$

b) $2x^2 - 20x$

$= 2(x^2 - 10x)$

$= 2[(x - 5)^2 - (-5)^2]$

$= 2[(x - 5)^2 - 25]$

6.

a) $x^2 + 2x - 8 = 0$

$(x^2 + 2x) = 8$

$(x + 1)^2 - 1 = 8$

$(x + 1)^2 = 9$

$x + 1 = \pm 3$

$x = \pm 3 - 1 \implies x = 2, -4$

b) $x^2 + 12x + 27 = 0$

$(x^2 + 12x) = -27$

$(x + 6)^2 - 36 = -27$

$(x + 6)^2 = 9$

$x + 6 = \pm 3$

$x = \pm 3 - 6 \implies x = -3, -9$

7. Using the formula:

$$x = \frac{-b \pm \sqrt{b^2 - 4ac}}{2a}$$

a) $2x^2 - 4x - 3 = 0$

$a = 2, b = -4, c = -3$

$$x = \frac{-b \pm \sqrt{b^2 - 4ac}}{2a}$$

$$= \frac{-(-4) \pm \sqrt{(-4)^2 - 4\,(2)(-3)}}{2(2)}$$

$$= \frac{4 \pm \sqrt{16 + 24}}{4}$$

$$= \frac{4 \pm 2\sqrt{10}}{4}$$

$$\therefore x = \frac{2 \pm \sqrt{10}}{2}$$

b) $x^2 - 2x - 4 = 0$

$a = 1, b = -2, c = -4$

$$x = \frac{-b \pm \sqrt{b^2 - 4ac}}{2a}$$

$$= \frac{-(-2) \pm \sqrt{(-2)^2 - 4\,(1)(-4)}}{2(1)}$$

$$= \frac{2 \pm \sqrt{4 + 16}}{2} = \frac{2 \pm 2\sqrt{5}}{2}$$

$$\therefore x = 1 \pm \sqrt{5}$$

6. INEQUALITIES

6.1 KEY POINTS

1. Notation on the Number line

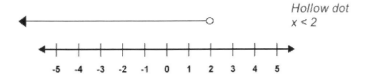

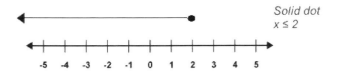

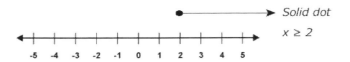

2. Linear Inequalities: (Learn by example)
    a) Find the set of values of x for

$$2x - 3 \leq 5$$

Solution:

Solve as a simple equation

$$2x - 3 \leq 5$$

$$2x \leq 5 + 3$$

$$2x \leq 8$$

$\therefore x \leq 4$ is the solution set.

    b) Find the set of values of x for

$$2(x + 4) < 9 + 3x$$

Solution:

Solve as a simple equation

$$2(x + 4) < 9 + 3x$$

$$2x + 8 < 9 + 3x$$

$$2x - 3x < 9 - 8$$

$$-x < 1$$

- Flip the inequality sign from < to >
- Change the signs of all terms

$\therefore x > -1$ is the solution set.

c) Find the set of values of x that satisfy the following

$$2x - 3 \leq 5 \text{ and } 2(x + 4) < 9 + 3x$$

From a. and b., we have the solution sets x ≤ 4 and

$x > -1$ a sketch describes the combined solution set

$-1 < x \le 4$

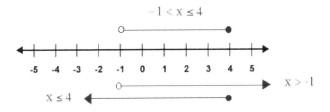

3. Quadratic Inequalities:
   a. Solve the quadratic equation.
   b. Sketch the graph.
   c. Use the sketch to find the solution.
      i)   For $y = f(x) > 0$, examine the graph above the x-axis.
      ii)   For $y = f(x) < 0$, examine the graph below the x-axis.

Example:

Find the set of values for x for which

$x^2 + x - 2 > 0$

a. Solve $x^2 + x - 2 = 0$

$(x + 2)(x - 1) = 0$

$x = 1, -2$

b. Sketch the graph.

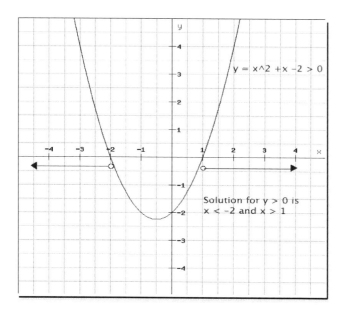

c. As $y = f(x) > 0$, examine the graph above the **x** - axis.

Solution set for $y > 0$ is $x < -2$ and $x > 1$

6.2 TEST YOURSELF

1. Using appropriate notation show the following linear inequalities on the number line.
   a) $x > -2$
   b) $x \leq 4$
   c) $-3 < x \leq 2$

2. Find the set of values of x that satisfy the following:

   $3x - 2 \geq 2x - 4$ and $2x + 3 < x + 4$

3. List 3 steps to solving a quadratic inequality.

4. Find the set of values for x for which

   $$x^2 + 2x - 3 < 0$$

6.3 ANSWERS

1.

a)

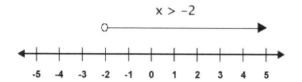

b)

c)

2. Simplifying the inequalities, we have:
$$3x - 2 \geq 2x - 4$$
$$3x - 2x \geq -4 + 2$$
$$x \geq -2$$
$$2x + 3 < x + 4$$
$$2x - x < 4 - 3$$
$$x < 1$$

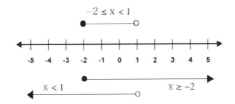

The solution set is $-2 \leq x < 1$

3. Check Key Points for answer.

4. $x^2 + 2x - 3 < 0$

   Solve $x^2 + 2x - 3 = 0$

   $(x + 3)(x - 1) = 0$

   $x = 1, -3$

   Sketch the graph $x^2 + 2x - 3 = 0$

   $y = x^2 + 2x - 3 < 0$

   For $y < 0$ we consider the graph below the $\textbf{x}$ axis.

   $x > -3$ and $x < 1$

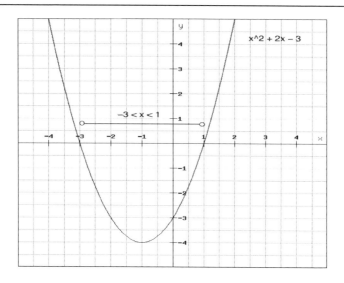

The solution set is $-3 < x < 1$

7. DISCRIMINANTS

7.1 KEY POINTS

1. The general form of a quadratic equation is:
    $f(x) = ax^2 + bx + c = 0$ where a, b and c are constants
    and $a \neq 0$.

2. The discriminant is given by $(b^2 - 4ac)$.
    If $b^2 - 4ac > 0$, the equation has 2 distinct roots.
    If $b^2 - 4ac = 0$, the equation has 2 equal roots.
    If $b^2 - 4ac < 0$, the equation has no roots.

3. Given $ax^2 + bx + c = 0$

    If $a > 0$, the curve is cup shaped. $\cup$

    If $a < 0$, the curve is bell shaped. $\cap$

4. The line of symmetry of the quadratic is given by the
    equation:

    $x = -\dfrac{b}{2}$ for $a = 1$

    In general , $x = -\dfrac{b}{2a}$

5. The coordinates of the vertex of the quadratic are

    $\left(-\dfrac{b}{2}, f\left(-\dfrac{b}{2}\right)\right)$ for $a = 1$

    $\left(-\dfrac{b}{2a}, f\left(-\dfrac{b}{2a}\right)\right)$ in general

6. Given the quadratic $y = x^2 + 3x - 4$, find the coordinates
    of the vertex and state the line of symmetry. Also find the

coordinates of all points where the graph $y = f(x)$ crosses the coordinate axes.

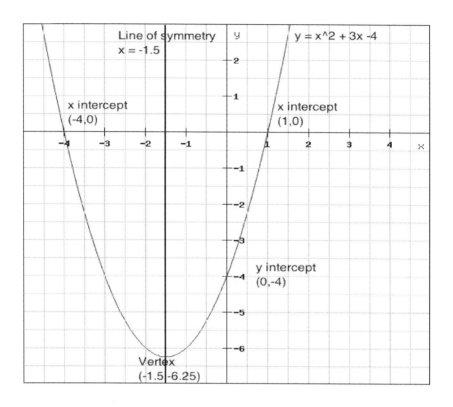

$x^2 + 3x - 4 = 0$
$(x + 4)(x - 1) = 0$
$\therefore x = 1, -4$
x intercepts are: $(1, 0)$ and $(-4, 0)$

If $x = 0; y = (0)^2 + 3(0) - 4 = -4$
y intercept is: $(0, -4)$

Line of symmetry is: $x = -\dfrac{b}{2} = -\dfrac{3}{2}$

If $x = -\frac{3}{2}$

$$y = \left(-\frac{3}{2}\right)^2 + 3\left(-\frac{3}{2}\right) - 4 = -\frac{25}{4}$$

Coordinates of vertex = $\left(-\frac{3}{2}, -\frac{25}{4}\right)$

7.2 TEST YOURSELF

1. Given a quadratic equation $ax^2 + bx + c = 0$, what is the discriminant?
2. If $b^2 - 4ac > 0$, the equation has _____roots.

   If $b^2 - 4ac = 0$, the equation has _____roots.

   If $b^2 - 4ac < 0$, the equation has _____roots.
3. Given $ax^2 + bx + c = 0$

   If $a > 0$, the curve is ___ shaped.

   If $a < 0$, the curve is ___ shaped.
4. What is the equation to the line of symmetry of a quadratic graph?
5. What are the coordinates of the vertex of a quadratic graph?
6. For $f(x) = x^2 - 2x - 3$
   a) Find the discriminant.
   b) Describe the roots.
   c) Is the graph bell shaped or cup shaped?
   d) Solve the quadratic and find the roots.
   e) State the line of symmetry.
   f) Find the coordinates of the vertex, the x-intercepts and the y-intercept of the graph

   g) Sketch the quadratic graph and mark the coordinates

   of x and y intercepts, the vertex and draw the line of

   symmetry.

7.3 ANSWERS

Questions 1-5: Check Key Points for answers.

6. For $f(x) = x^2 - 2x - 3$
    a) $a = 1\ b = -2, c = -3$
        $\therefore$ the discriminant $= b^2 - 4ac$
        $= (-2)^2 - 4(1)(-3)$
        $= 4 + 12 = 16$
        $b^2 - 4ac = 16 > 0$
        $\therefore$ the equation has 2 distinct roots.
    b) $a = 1 > 0$, hence the curve is cup shaped. $\cup$
    c) $x^2 - 2x - 3 = 0$

        $(x - 3)(x + 1) = 0$

        $x = 3, -1$ are the roots of the equation

    d) The line of symmetry is:
        $$x = -\frac{b}{2} = -\frac{(-2)}{2} = 1$$
        $x = 1$
    e) The coordinates of the vertex of the graph are
        $(-\frac{b}{2}, f(-\frac{b}{2}))$
        $$-\frac{b}{2} = 1$$
        $$f(-\frac{b}{2}) = \left(-\frac{b}{2}\right)^2 - 2\left(-\frac{b}{2}\right) - 3$$
        $= 1 - 2 - 3 = -4$
        Coordinates of vertex = (1, -4)

        Coordinates of x −intercepts are: (3, 0) and (-1, 0).

        Coordinates of y −intercept are found by putting

        $x = 0$ in $y = x^2 - 2x - 3 = -3$

        (0, -3) is the y-intercept.

f)   Sketching the graph $y = x^2 - 2x - 3$

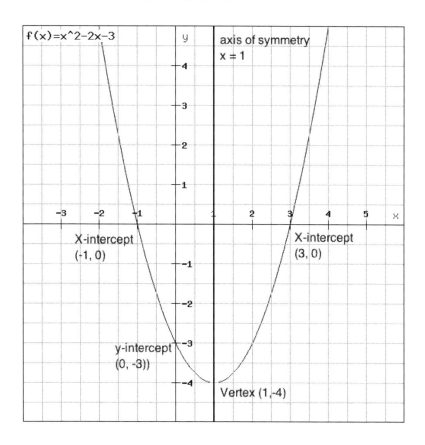

8. SKETCHING ALGEBRAIC GRAPHS

8.1 KEY POINTS

1.
   a) Sketching the quadratic equation $y = x^2$

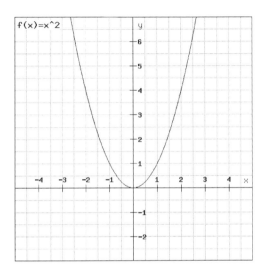

   b) Sketching the quadratic equation $y = -x^2$

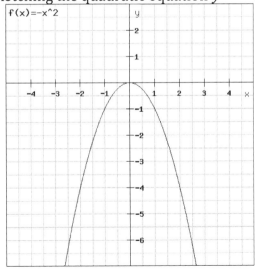

2.

   a) Sketching the cubic equation $y = x^3$

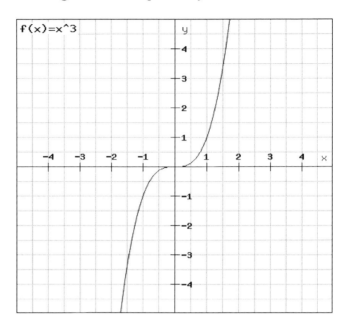

b) Sketching the cubic equation $y = -x^3$

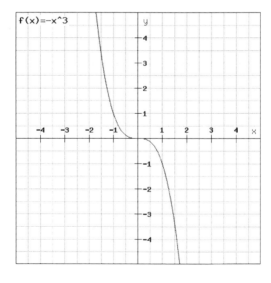

3.

Sketching the Cubic Equation
$$y = (x - a)(x - b)(x - c)$$

If $y = 0$;

$x = a, b, c$

If $x = 0$;

$y = -abc$

Example:

$$y = f(x) = (x - 1)(x - 2)(x - 3)$$

If $y = 0$;

$x = 1, 2, 3$

If $x = 0$;

$y = -abc$

$= -(1)(2)(3) = -6$

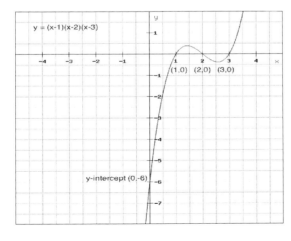

4.
a)   Sketching Reciprocal graphs

$$y = \frac{1}{x}, y = \frac{2}{x}, y = \frac{3}{x}$$

The $x - axis$ is the horizontal asymptote.

The $y - axis$ is the vertical asymptote.

$$y = \frac{1}{x}$$

When $x = 1, y = 1$

When $y = 1, x = 1$

$$y = \frac{2}{x}$$

When $x = 2, y = 1$

When $y = 2, x = 1$

$$y = \frac{3}{x}$$

When $x = 3, y = 1$

When $y = 3, x = 1$

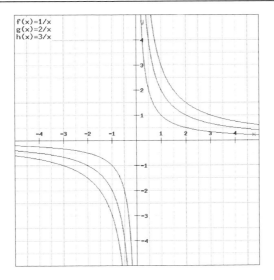

b)   Sketching Reciprocal graphs

$$y = -\frac{1}{x}, y = -\frac{2}{x}, y = -\frac{3}{x}$$

The $x - axis$ is the horizontal asymptote.

The $y - axis$ is the vertical asymptote.

$$y = -\frac{1}{x}$$

When $x = 1, y = -1$

When $y = 1, x = -1$

$$y = -\frac{2}{x}$$

When $x = 2, y = -1$

When $y = 2, x = -1$

$$y = -\frac{3}{x}$$

When $x = 3, y = -1$

When $y = 3, x = -1$

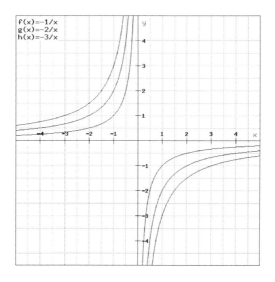

5.

a) Sketching the Square root graph $y = \sqrt{x}$

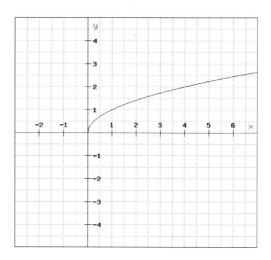

b) Sketching the Square root graph $y = -\sqrt{x}$

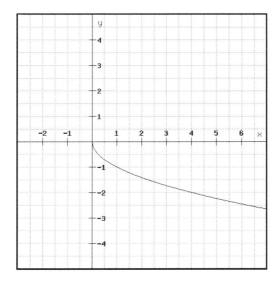

8.2 TEST YOURSELF

1.

a) Sketch the quadratic equation $y = x^2$

b) Sketch the quadratic equation $y = -x^2$

2.

a) Sketch the cubic equation $y = x^3$

b) Sketch the cubic equation $y = -x^3$

3.

Sketch the cubic equation $y = x^3 - 4x$

Mark and label the **x** and **y** intercepts.

4.

a) Sketch the reciprocal graph $y = \frac{1}{x}$

b) Sketch the reciprocal graph $y = -\frac{1}{x}$

5.

a) Sketch the square root graph

$$y = \sqrt{x}$$

b) Sketch the square root graph

$$y = -\sqrt{x}$$

8.3 ANSWERS

1. Check Key points for answer.

2. Check Key points for answer.

3. Sketch of cubic function $y = x^3 - 4x$

$y = x(x^2 - 4)$

$y = x(x + 2)(x - 2)$

x -intercepts are $(-2,0), (0,0)$ and $(2,0)$

y -intercept is $(0,0)$

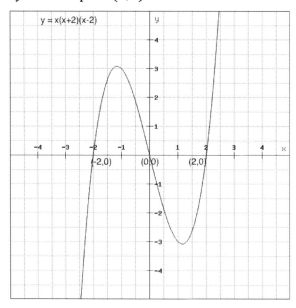

4. Check Key Points for answer.

5. Check Key Points for answer.

9. TRANSFORMATIONS OF ALGEBRAIC GRAPHS

9.1 KEY POINTS

1.
$$y_1 = f(x_1)$$
$$y_2 = f(x_2 + a)$$
This is a horizontal translation of $- a$ in the x direction.

$$(x_2, y_2) = (x_1 - a, y_1)$$

Example:

Apply the transformation $f(x + 2)$ to the curve

$$f(x) = x^2$$

Sketch the curves $f(x)$ and $f(x + 2)$.

$$y = f(x) = x^2$$

$$y = f(x + 2) = (x + 2)^2$$

Using $(x_2, y_2) = (x_1 - 2, y_1)$, we transform

points on curve $f(x)$ to points on curve $f(x + 2)$.

$$(0,0) \Rightarrow (-2,0)$$

$$(2,4) \Rightarrow (0,4)$$

$$(-2,4) \Rightarrow (-4,4)$$

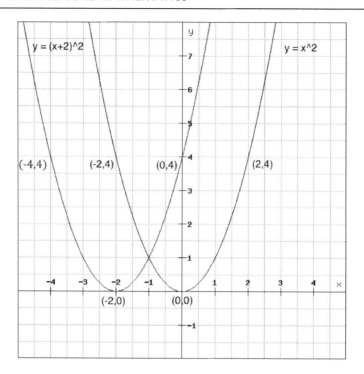

This is a horizontal translation of – 2 in the x direction.

2. $y_1 = f(x_1)$
    $y_2 = f(x_2) + a$

This is a vertical translation of $+a$ in the y direction.

$$(x_2, y_2) = (x_1, y_1 + a)$$

Example:

Apply the transformation

$$f(x) + 3$$

to the curve
$$f(x) = x^2$$

Sketch the curves $f(x)$ and

$f(x) + 3$

$y = f(x) = x^2$

$y = f(x) + 3 = x^2 + 3$

Using $(x_2, y_2) = (x_1, y_1 + 3)$, we transform

points on curve $f(x)$ to points on curve $f(x) + 3$

$(0,0) \Rightarrow (0,3)$

$(2,4) \Rightarrow (2,7)$

$(-2,4) \Rightarrow (-2,7)$

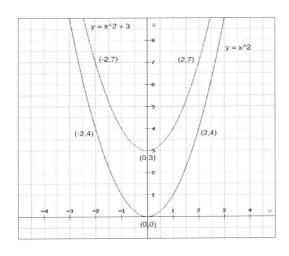

This is a vertical translation of $+3$ in the y direction.

3. $y_1 = f(x_1)$

$$y_2 = f(ax_2)$$

This is a horizontal stretch of $\frac{1}{a}$ in the x direction.

$$(x_2, y_2) = (\frac{x_1}{a}, y_1)$$

Example:

Apply the transformation $f(2x)$

to the curve $f(x) = x^2$

Sketch the curves $f(x)$ and $f(2x)$

$$y = f(x) = x^2$$

$$y = f(2x) = (2x)^2$$

Using $(x_2, y_2) = (\frac{x_1}{2}, y_1)$

we transform points on curve $f(x)$

to points on curve $f(2x)$

$$(0,0) \Rightarrow (0,0)$$

$$(2,4) \Rightarrow (1,4)$$

$$(-2,4) \Rightarrow (-1,4)$$

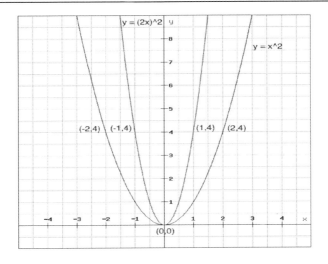

This is a horizontal stretch of $+\frac{1}{2}$ in the x direction.

4. $y_1 = f(x_1)$
    $y_2 = af(x_2)$
    This is a vertical stretch of $+a$ in the y direction.

    $(x_2, y_2) = (x_1, ay_1)$

Example:

Apply the transformation $2f(x)$ to the curve

$f(x) = x^2$

Sketch the curves $f(x)$ and $2f(x)$.

$y = f(x) = x^2$

$y = 2f(x) = 2x^2$

Using $(x_2, y_2) = (x_1, 2y_1)$, we transform

points on curve $f(x)$ to points on curve $2f(x)$.

$(0,0) \Rightarrow (0,0)$

$(2,4) \Rightarrow (2,8)$

$(-2,4) \Rightarrow (-2,8)$

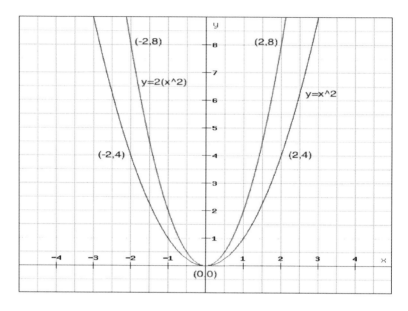

This is a vertical stretch of $+2$ in the y direction.

5. $y_1 = f(x_1)$

$y_2 = f(-x_2)$

This is a reflection in the y axis.

$(x_2, y_2) = (-x_1, y_1)$

6. $y_1 = f(x_1)$

$y_2 = -f(x_2)$

This is a reflection in the x axis.

$(x_2, y_2) = (x_1, -y_1)$

9.2 TEST YOURSELF

1. Describe the transformation of curve $y_1 = f(x_1)$
   to curve $y_2 = f(x_2 + a)$.

   What is $(x_2, y_2) =$
2. Describe the transformation of curve $y_1 = f(x_1)$
   to curve $y_2 = f(x_2) + a$
   What is $(x_2, y_2) =$
3. Describe the transformation of curve $y_1 = f(x_1)$
   to curve $y_2 = f(ax_2)$
   What is $(x_2, y_2) =$
4. Describe the transformation of curve $y_1 = f(x_1)$
   to curve $y_2 = af(x_2)$
   What is $(x_2, y_2) =$
5. Describe the transformation of curve $y_1 = f(x_1)$
   to curve $y_2 = f(-x_2)$
   What is $(x_2, y_2) =$
6. Describe the transformation of curve $y_1 = f(x_1)$
   to curve $y_2 = -f(x_2)$
   What is $(x_2, y_2) =$
7. If $(2,2)$ is a point on the curve $y = f(x)$
   What does the point transform to on the following
   transformed curves?
   Describe each transformation.
   a) $y = 3f(x)$
   b) $y = f(5x)$
   c) $y = f(x) - 4$
   d) $y = f(x - 2)$

9.3 ANSWERS

Questions 1-6: Check Key Points for answers.

7.
a) $y = 3f(x)$

This is a vertical stretch of 3 in the y direction.

$$(x_2, y_2) = (x_1, 3y_1)$$
$$\therefore (2,2) \Rightarrow (2,6)$$

b) $y = f(5x)$

This is a horizontal stretch of $\frac{1}{5}$ in the x direction.

$$(x_2, y_2) = (\frac{x_1}{5}, y_1)$$
$$\therefore (2,2) \Rightarrow (\frac{2}{5}, 2)$$

c) $y = f(x) - 4$

This is a vertical translation of -4 in the y direction.

$$(x_2, y_2) = (x_1, y_1 - 4)$$
$$\therefore (2,2) \Rightarrow (2, -2)$$

d) $y = f(x - 2)$

This is a horizontal translation of $+2$ in the x direction.

$$(x_2, y_2) = (x_1 + 2, y_1)$$
$$\therefore (2,2) \Rightarrow (4,2)$$

10. DIFFERENTIATION

10.1 KEY POINTS

1. The first order derivative $f'(x)$ is the slope or gradient of a curve $y = f(x)$ at a point on the curve. $f'(x)$ is the slope of the tangent at any point on the curve.
    - If $y = f(x) = x^n$

    $$\frac{dy}{dx} = f'(x) = nx^{n-1}$$

    Example: $y = x^{\frac{1}{2}}$

    $$\frac{dy}{dx} = \frac{1}{2}x^{\frac{1}{2}-1} = \frac{1}{2}x^{-\frac{1}{2}} = \frac{1}{2x^{\frac{1}{2}}}$$

    - If $y = f(x) = ax^n$

    $$\frac{dy}{dx} = f'(x) = nax^{n-1}$$

    Example: $y = 3x^4 - 5x^2$

    $$\frac{dy}{dx} = 12x^3 - 10x$$

2. The second order derivative $f''(x) = \frac{d^2y}{dx^2}$ is the derivative of the derivative $f'(x)$ and denotes the concavity or convexity of the curve.

3. Stationary Points

    When the gradient or slope of the curve is 0, the curve is at a stationary point.

a) The stationary point is a maximum point.

$\frac{dy}{dx} = 0$ and $\frac{d^2y}{dx^2} < 0$

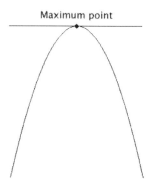

Maximum point

b) The stationary point is a minimum point.

$\frac{dy}{dx} = 0$ and $\frac{d^2y}{dx^2} > 0$

Minimum point

c) The stationary point is an inflexion point.

$\frac{dy}{dx} = 0$ and $\frac{d^2y}{dx^2} = 0$

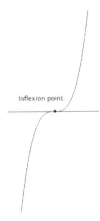

4. In order to find the coordinates of the stationary points of a graph:

   a. Equate $\frac{dy}{dx}$ to 0 and solve the function.

   b. For each x, find the corresponding y.

   c. Compute $\frac{d^2y}{dx^2}$ for each x.

   - If $\frac{d^2y}{dx^2} < 0$, the stationary point is a maximum point.
   - If $\frac{d^2y}{dx^2} > 0$, the stationary point is a minimum point.
   - If $\frac{d^2y}{dx^2} = 0$, the stationary point is an inflexion point.

10.2 TEST YOURSELF

1. Define the first order derivative of a curve $y = f(x)$

2. Given that $y = f(x) = x^n$,

   the first order derivative $\frac{dy}{dx} = f'(x) =$

3. Given that $y = f(x) = ax^n$,

   the first order derivative $\frac{dy}{dx} = f'(x) =$

4. Define the second order derivative of a curve $y = f(x)$.

5. Define a stationary point.

6. Name, sketch and describe 3 stationary points.

7. Describe the 3 steps to finding the coordinates of the stationary points of a curve and determining their nature.

8. Given that $y = \frac{1}{3}x^3 - 16x$

   a. Find $f'(x)$.

   b. Find $f''(x)$

   c. What are the coordinates of the stationary points?

   d. Determine whether the stationary points are maximum or minimum points.

10.3 ANSWERS

Questions 1-7: Check Key Points for answers.

8. $y = f(x) = \frac{1}{3}x^3 - 16x$

  a) $f'(x) = 3.\frac{1}{3}x^2 - 16$

   $= x^2 - 16$

  b) $f''(x) = \frac{d}{dx}(x^2 - 16)$

   $= 2x$

  c) <u>Step 1</u>: Equate $f'(x)$ to 0 and solve.

   $x^2 - 16 = 0$

   $(x + 4)(x - 4) = 0$

   $x = 4, -4$

   <u>Step 2</u>: For each x, find y.

   $y = f(x) = \frac{1}{3}x^3 - 16x$

   $f(4) \quad = \frac{1}{3}(4)^3 - 16(4)$

   $= \frac{64}{3} - 64$

$$= \frac{(64 - 192)}{3}$$

$$= \frac{-128}{3}$$

$$f(-4) = \frac{1}{3}(-4)^3 - 16(-4)$$

$$= -\frac{64}{3} + 64$$

$$= \frac{(-64 + 192)}{3}$$

$$= \frac{128}{3}$$

$(4, \frac{-128}{3})$ and $(-4, \frac{128}{3})$ are the stationary points.

d) We compute $\frac{d^2y}{dx^2}$ for each x:

$$\frac{d^2y}{dx^2} = 2x$$

For $\left(4, \frac{-128}{3}\right)$,

$$\frac{d^2y}{dx^2} = 2(4) = 8 > 0$$

$$\frac{d^2y}{dx^2} > 0$$

$\Rightarrow$ Stationary Point $\left(4, \frac{-128}{3}\right)$

is a minimum point.

For $\left(-4, \frac{128}{3}\right)$

$\frac{d^2y}{dx^2} = 2(-4) = -8 < 0$

$\frac{d^2y}{dx^2} < 0$

$\Rightarrow$ Stationary Point $\left(-4, \frac{128}{3}\right)$

is a maximum point.

11. COORDINATE GEOMETRY - LINES

11.1 KEY POINTS

1. Distance Formula

The distance between two points (x_1, y_1) and (x_2, y_2)

$$d = \sqrt{(x_1 - x_2)^2 + (y_1 - y_2)^2}$$

2. Midpoint Formula

The coordinates of the midpoint of a line joining the points

(x_1, y_1) and (x_2, y_2)

$$\text{Midpoint} = (\frac{x_1 + x_2}{2}, \frac{y_1 + y_2}{2})$$

3. Slope Formula

The slope or gradient of a line joining points (x_1, y_1) and

(x_2, y_2)

$$m = \frac{(y_1 - y_2)}{(x_1 - x_2)}$$

4. The equation of a straight line in general form is

$ax + by + c = 0$ where a, b and c are integers.

5. The equation of a line with slope m and y-intercept c is $y = mx + c$

6. The equation of a line with gradient m and passing through the point (x_1, y_1) is

    $$y - y_1 = m(x - x_1)$$

7. The equation of a line passing through two points (x_1, y_1) and (x_2, y_2).

    $$\frac{(y - y_1)}{(y_2 - y_1)} = \frac{(x - x_1)}{(x_2 - x_1)}$$

8. If the gradient of a line is m, the gradient of a line parallel to it is also m.

9. If the gradient of a line is m, the gradient of a line perpendicular to it is $-\frac{1}{m}$.

10. If two lines are perpendicular the product of their gradients $= -1$.

11. If a line intersects the x-axis, put $y = 0$ in the equation to get the coordinates of intersection as $(x, 0)$ the x - intercept.

12. If a line intersects the y-axis, put $x = 0$ in the equation to get the coordinates of intersection as $(0, y)$ the y-intercept.

11.2 TEST YOURSELF

1. State the Distance Formula.

   The distance between two points (x_1, y_1) and $(x_2, y_2) =$

2. State the Midpoint Formula.

   The coordinates of the midpoint of a line joining the points

   (x_1, y_1) and (x_2, y_2) are

3. State the Slope Formula

   The slope or gradient of a line joining points and (x_2, y_2)

   is(x_1, y_1)

4. State the general form of the equation to a straight line.

5. State the equation of a line with slope m and y-intercept c.

6. State the equation of a line with gradient m and passing

   through the point (x_1, y_1).

7. State the equation of a line passing through two points

   (x_1, y_1) and (x_2, y_2).

8. If the gradient of a line is m, the gradient of a line parallel

   to it is_____.

   If the gradient of a line is m, the gradient of a line

   perpendicular to it is _____.

   If two lines are perpendicular the product of their

   gradients =_____.

9. How do you find the y – intercept of a line?

10. How do you find the x – intercept of a line?

11. Calculate the distance between the points (2, -5) and (-6, 1).

12. What is the midpoint of the line joining the points (3, 2) and (5, -6)?

13. What is the slope of the line joining the points (4, -1) and (2, -5)?

14. Find the equation of the line with a gradient of -3 and an intercept on the y – axis at (0, 2).

15. Find the equation of the line with gradient 4 and passing through the point (2, -1).

16. Find the equation of the line passing through the points (-2, 8) and (-12, 3).

17. Find the equation of the line that passes through the point (-1, 3) and parallel to the line $y = 5x - 3$.

18. Find the equation of the line that passes through the point (5, -2) and perpendicular to the line $y = \frac{3}{2}x - 1$.

11.3 ANSWERS

Questions 1-10: Check Key Points for answers.

11. $d = \sqrt{(x_2 - x_1)^2 + (y_2 - y_1)^2}$

Distance between the points $(2, -5)$ and $(-6, 1)$

$= \sqrt{(2 - (-6))^2 + (-5 - 1)^2}$

$= \sqrt{(8)^2 + (-6)^2}$

$= \sqrt{64 + 36}$

$= \sqrt{100} = 10$

12. Midpoint $= (\frac{x_1 + x_2}{2}, \frac{y_1 + y_2}{2})$

The midpoint of the line joining the points $(3, 2)$ and

$(5, -6)$

$= (\frac{3 + 5}{2}, \frac{2 + (-6)}{2})$

$= (\frac{8}{2}, \frac{-4}{2}) = (4, -2)$

13. $m = \frac{(y_1 - y_2)}{(x_1 - x_2)}$

The slope of the line joining the points $(4, -1)$ and $(2, -5)$

$$= \frac{(-1-(-5))}{(4-2)}$$

$$= 2$$

14. $y = mx + c$

The equation of the line with gradient -3 and

y-intercept $(0, 2)$ is

$$y = (-3)x + 2$$

$$y = -3x + 2$$

15. $y - y_1 = m(x - x_1)$

The equation of the line with gradient 4 and passing

through the point $(2, -1)$ is

$$y - (-1) = 4(x - 2)$$

$$y + 1 = 4x - 8$$

$$y = 4x - 9$$

16. $\frac{(y-y_1)}{(y_2-y_1)} = \frac{(x-x_1)}{(x_2-x_1)}$

The equation of the line passing through the points $(-2, 8)$

and $(-12, 3)$ is

$$\frac{(y-8)}{(3-8)} = \frac{(x-(-2))}{(-12-(-2))}$$

$$\frac{(y-8)}{(-5)} = \frac{(x+2)}{(-10)}$$

$$-10(y-8) = -5(x+2)$$

$$-10y + 80 = -5x - 10$$

$$5x - 10y + 90 = 0$$

$$x - 2y + 18 = 0$$

17. $y - y_1 = m(x - x_1)$

Slope of the line $y = 5x - 3$ is 5.

The equation of the line that passes through the point

(-1, 3) with slope also 5 is

$$y - 3 = 5(x - (-1))$$

$$y - 3 = 5(x + 1)$$

$$y - 3 = 5x + 5$$

$$5x - y + 8 = 0$$

18. $y - y_1 = m(x - x_1)$

Slope of the line $y = \frac{3}{2}x - 1$ is $\frac{3}{2}$

$\therefore$ Slope of a line perpendicular to it is $-\frac{2}{3}$

The equation of the line that passes the point

(5, -2) and perpendicular to the line $y = \frac{3}{2}x - 1$

is $y - (-2) = -\frac{2}{3}(x - 5)$

$y + 2 = -\frac{2}{3}(x - 5)$

$3(y + 2) = -2x + 10$

$3y + 6 = -2x + 10$

$2x + 3y - 4 = 0$

12. COORDINATE GEOMETRY – CIRCLES

12.1 KEY POINTS

1. Standard Form:

   The equation of a circle with centre (a, b) and radius r is given by

   $$(x - a)^2 + (y - b)^2 = r^2$$

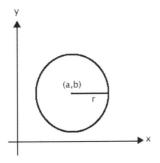

2. General Form:

   The equation of a circle in general form is given by

   $$x^2 + y^2 + Ax + By + C = 0$$

   Use completing the square on x and y to convert it to standard form.

   $$(x^2 + Ax) + (y^2 + By) = -C$$

3. The equation of a circle with centre at origin is given by

   $$x^2 + y^2 = r^2$$

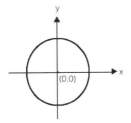

4. Tangents and Normals

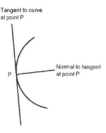

Tangents and Normals are straight lines perpendicular to each other.

5. The (slope of the tangent)×(slope of the normal) $= -1$ at a particular point.

6. The equation of a tangent to a curve at a point (x_1, y_1) is given by the equation $y - y_1 = m(x - x_1)$ where the gradient m of the tangent is computed from the $\frac{dy}{dx}$ of the curve at $x = x_1$

7. The equation of a normal to a curve at a point (x_1, y_1) is given by the equation $y - y_1 = m_1(x - x_1)$ where the gradient m_1 of the normal is computed from the gradient m of the tangent at $x = x_1$, $m_1 = -\frac{1}{m}$

8. The coordinates of the point of intersection of a tangent and a curve can be found by equating the equation of the tangent with the equation of the curve.

12.2 TEST YOURSELF

1. State the equation of a circle with centre (a, b) and radius r.

2. State the equation of a circle in general form.

3. State the equation of a circle with centre at the origin.

4. The slope of the tangent $\times$ slope of the normal $=$ _____ at a particular point.

5. How is the gradient of a tangent computed at a point (x_1, y_1) of a curve $y = f(x)$?

6. How are the coordinates of the point of intersection of a tangent and a curve found?

7. Write down the equation of the circle with centre $(2, -6)$ and radius 4.

8. Write down the coordinates of the centre and the radius of the circle with equation:

$$(x - 3)^2 + (x + 2)^2 = 16$$

9. Write down the equation of the circle with centre at the origin and radius $\sqrt{3}$

10. Find the coordinates of the centre and the radius of the circle with equation

$$x^2 + y^2 + 6x - 2y - 6 = 0$$

11. A curve has the equation

$$3x^2 - 2x.$$

a) Find the gradient of the curve at the point for which $x = 1$.

b) Find the equation of the normal to the curve at the point for which $x = 1$

12. The line $y = 3x + 4$ meets the circle

$x^2 + y^2 + 6x - 4y - 4 = 0$ at two points A and B.

Find the coordinates of A and B.

12.3 ANSWERS

Questions 1-6: Check Key Points for answers.

7. $(x-a)^2 + (y-b)^2 = r^2$

The equation of the circle with centre (2, -6) and radius 4

is

$(x-2)^2 + (y-(-6))^2 = 4^2$

$(x-2)^2 + (y+6)^2 = 16$

8. $(x-3)^2 + (x+2)^2 = 16$

Coordinates of centre $= (3, -2)$

Radius $= \sqrt{16} = 4$

9. $x^2 + y^2 = r^2$

The equation of the circle with centre at the origin and

radius $\sqrt{3}$ is

$x^2 + y^2 = \sqrt{3}^2$

$x^2 + y^2 = 3$

10. $x^2 + y^2 + 6x - 2y - 6 = 0$

$$(x^2 + 6x) + (y^2 - 2y) = 6$$

Completing the square for x and y,

$$[(x + 3)^2 - 9] + [(y - 1)^2 - 1] = 6$$

$$[(x + 3)^2] + [(y - 1)^2] = 6 + 9 + 1$$

$$(x + 3)^2 + (y - 1)^2 = 16$$

Radius $= \sqrt{16} = 4$

Coordinates of centre $= (-3, 1)$

11. $y = 3x^2 - 2x$

i)$\frac{dy}{dx} = 6x - 2$

Gradient of the curve at the point $x = 1$

$$\frac{dy}{dx} = 6x - 2$$

$$= 6(1) - 2 = 4$$

ii) At point $x = 1$, $y = 3x^2 - 2x$

$$\therefore y = 3(1)^2 - 2(1) = 3 - 2 = 1$$

Gradient of the normal at the point $(1, 1) = -\frac{1}{4}$

∴ the equation of the normal to the curve at the point

(1,1) is

$$(y - 1) = -\frac{1}{4}(x - 1)$$

$$4(y - 1) = -x + 1$$

$$4y - 4 + x - 1 = 0$$

$x + 4y - 5 = 0$ is the required equation of the normal.

12. Line: $y = 3x + 4$

Circle: $x^2 + y^2 + 6x - 4y - 4 = 0$

Substituting $y = 3x + 4$ in equation to the circle,

$$x^2 + (3x + 4)^2 + 6x - 4(3x + 4) - 4 = 0$$

$$x^2 + 9x^2 + 24x + 16 + 6x - 12x - 16 - 4 = 0$$

$$10x^2 + 18x - 4 = 0$$

$$5x^2 + 9x - 2 = 0$$

$$(5x - 1)(x + 2) = 0$$

$$x = -2, x = \frac{1}{5}$$

For $x = -2, y = 3x + 4$

$y = 3(-2) + 4 = -6 + 4 = -2$

Point A $(-2, -2)$

For $x = \frac{1}{5}$

$y = 3x + 4$

$y = 3\left(\frac{1}{5}\right) + 4$

$= \frac{3}{5} + 4 = \frac{23}{5}$

Point B $(\frac{1}{5}, \frac{23}{5})$

ABOUT THE AUTHOR

Shobha Natarajan holds an MSc in Mathematics from Bangalore University and teaches Mathematics to students at A Level and GCSE in the Medway area of Kent. The Maths Clinic was established in 2011 to publish revision guides in Mathematics in print and Kindle e-book format. These books would soon be available as mobile apps on Apple iOS and Android devices. Shobha is a software professional with over 25 years' experience in embedded software development.

www.themathsclinic.co.uk

Printed in Great Britain
by Amazon